After
Small apple trees

Peter Hámor

BookLeaf Publishing

India | USA | UK

Presentation by *BookLeaf Publishing*

Web: www.bookleafpub.com

E-mail: info@bookleafpub.com

ISBN: 9789358317695

First edition 2023

ACKNOWLEDGEMENT

Yared, you saved me.

I will never forgive you for that.

Minutes after

What's never begun
has no right to end.

Not like this.

Day one

Never again
will I be able to bring you boxes with pizza,
will I?
Make your joints crack in relief
Wash your back in the shower
Fall asleep actively ignoring the movie
we spent more than an hour picking

Never again
will I be woken up by fever-dreams-driven
instructions on how to perform lumbar punctures
(tonight, in french)

In the end
You realized what actually matters to you.
It was not the fresh tea
Or the long, cozy evenings
Or the joy
Even though you brought so much of it into my
life

We were so happy
But you said it's difficult to love two people at
the same time

So you didn't

Day two

If love could be selfish
I would hold you
and tell you everything
that you've helped me become

But you knew

And still
It was not me

Day four

The air still smells of concrete
The sun still makes my tattoos slowly fade
You are slowly beginning to fade, too.
I hate it.

I'll glue what's left of me
with gold

Day five

You talk to me
Like we're still us

Yet every night
you're in someone else's arms

Happy
Secure
Loved

How little you must care
Thinking I don't imagine you
With her

How little you must care
To talk to me like we're still us
So you feel better about leaving

Day seven

Under different stars
I would read you papers
And you would be excited
for our future

I do believe
That some lives are meant to be spent unloved

Day eleven

Now I know
That I don't grieve losing you
But what never came to be

Blinded
by how softly you touched me
For a moment
stopping the pain

And then
when I reached out my hands
You kissed me
Smiled
And left

The sweet and jagged pain
Of losing something that's never started
Feels like waking up into a rainy morning
From a dream that had too many colors

Now I know
It was not real

Now, I know
The depth and extent of me

One day
I'll reach out my hands again
And maybe someone will take them
Smile
And stay

Today

Today you told me you got engaged.

I helped you move to a different city
We mounted your cabinets
Decorated your living room

Built your bed.

There's so much light in your new home

Today
I met your fiance.

She is amazing.

And I finally understand
Why it could have never been me

Waves

A sea of color
Both bright and dark

Your ship on its way to the already pre-charted
shores
While mine always heads to the unknown

We were so lucky
that the ocean brought us together.

Even if we were
just for a single storm
and a few sunny days

I can already see your shores.

I can see your sails getting smaller with every
rain.

I know you'll make it there safe
And I will once again
disappear in the mist.

The Sun

If I died
in this very moment
no heart would be broken
no mourning would take place
no regrets would emerge

Just as the Sun's sudden death
It would take some time for people to notice

They would shrug
Sigh
And go on

Because unlike Sun's light
there's no need for me to exist
for anyone else to keep on living.

Bruises

It's been months
that I've been asking myself
Why?

Why on some days
the muscles right below my collarbones
hurt

I test all possible movements
Lift everything I can hold onto
Just to find the culprit of this pain

Some days
bruises appear out of nowhere
And I keep second-guessing my sanity.
Could they be self-inflicted?

Last night
I'm once again looking into your eyes
while you're breathing heavily into me.

And then I felt it.
The familiar pain of your forearms
burying into the flesh right below my
collarbones
as the weight of your body
helped the sheets swallow me whole

Letting go

I have to let you go
Before I get to touch your beautiful back again
Kiss your neck
Make you breakfast
Listen to your stories of amazing places I wish I
could visit with you one day

You said you love me
and then kissed someone else

So I have to let you go
Before I've ever gotten the chance to tell you
How much I wanted us

In three days

I'm going to die.

I brought snacks
I entertain
I drink
I pretend I'm alive

There's so little left of me
that I doubt there has ever been anything other
than the heaviness

I see you all
Living
And I'm so jealous
I envy all your feelings

All of them.

Some lives are not meant to be lived in
happiness

It hurts
But there's nothing more I can do
Other than keeping on suffering
Or leave

Funny how things that make us the strongest
are the same things that break us into the finest
dust.

In a few days
I'll be free

It's too late

17

I wish we'd met
when there was still hope for me

Home

How beautiful is this field of grass
Seen from below
I can't hear rustling of leaves
Instead
I feel every root growing
Throughout my remains
I've become the tree
On which your children climb

We were told that eternity feels like a single
moment
And yet, here I still am, deep in unsleep
Moving with the ground.
The more apart I'm torn
The more I'm a part of the earth
Gently washed away by the rain
Saved by rivers

You'll always find me in the ocean.
I had never left.

Crossroads

I stood by the road
with nowhere to go
So scared that you'll see me alone and lost
Yet I gathered the rest of my courage
All the hope that was left
And looked back

Your absence reminded me
That I truly am

Despare ribs

That's it, my love.

That was the last time I tore my chest open
So you could see how much love for you there is
inside me
Filling the spaces between my broken ribs
Pouring out not in waves
But in steady, harsh rapids.

I'm so glad I opened my heart to you one more
time
Because your hands
again
were not there to catch the waterfall
And so, as every river without rain
The love has dried up

That's it, my love.

After the universe

And for one night
I allow myself to be happy

Hope

There are so many poems I wrote about you

I hope you'll never get to read them

I don't want you to know how much I loved you

Because then you'd finally know
Everything

Watching

I haven't let you go. I never will.
But I stopped holding you inside me.
I gave you all the love I had
and opened my arms.
Because now I know that true love doesn't cage.

There's a piece of my soul that bears your name
and that part of me will love you forever.

I shine

Sometimes
a silver lining
is an event horizon.

www.ingramcontent.com/pod-product-compliance
Lightning Source LLC
LaVergne TN
LVHW021346200726

843509LV00014B/2698